Introduction

I started in marketing at the tender age of twenty-two. At that time, I started a mobile Notary Public business.

I realized nobody was going to "beat a path to my door," as that old quote says. And it dawned on me-in order for people to know about my service, I needed to get the word out.

The question was, how would I get the word out when I didn't have any money? I was living with my parents at the time, not paying any rent and noticed that other mobile notaries advertised.

I looked in the yellow pages, online, googled. Did the whole research thing and it became apparent that some notaries were doing well and others were not doing well.

So I went on a quest to learn how to effectively market my business. Yellow pages, online, hand out my cards to everybody. There were various methods.

But I also realized that, in order for people to find out about my service, I needed to do something. I couldn't sit at home and surf the web or play video games or watch television or just roam around in my pajamas and expect people to call and hire me.

First thing I did was post an advertisement in the Yellow Pages that generated some calls. Then posted some advertisements on line; I didn't know anything about key words, pay-per-click, SEO, but started to get some calls from that, too.

Then I advertised in some other places and got calls. Well, by year's end 2006, at the young age of only twenty-two, I earned a decent livelihood of thirty thousand dollars. And this was not working sixty hours a week or killing myself running all over town.

This was simply living on my terms. I didn't know how to budget or save so I didn't have much to show for it. When I wasn't doing an assignment, I was at the movies or hanging out or driving around randomly or even shopping (I like to shop).

Being so young, knowing that a series of checks totalling a thousand dollars had just arrived from jobs I did recently, knowing I had little to no overhead, would cause anybody to want to go out and shop. So at ten or eleven AM I'd be in the mall.

But it became clear to me that if I were to keep the well of revenue running, I needed to continue marketing myself. Which differentiates business owners from employees.

Employees don't need to market themselves to earn a pay check. Business owners on the other hand, need to kick our rear ends into high gear, or the well runs dry. So I found out that I enjoyed marketing.

I didn't necessarily enjoy the interaction with people, although I do like meeting people and getting to know them and that kind of thing.

But I didn't enjoy the work, you know, going out and developing writer's cramp and travelling to people's houses, not knowing what to expect. Most people are nice enough.

But sometimes I'd arrive late and get an earful. I didn't like that aspect of it, but the marketing was great! It was a joy to post an advertisement online or in the Yellow Pages and see results from my ad.

A couple years later, I really delved into marketing. It was around 2007 and I was doing the mobile notary business in addition to helping my Dad with his CPA practice.

The CPA practice is a bit different from the mobile notary business because in the CPA practice my dad is the boss. So it was challenging.

But once we got over that hurdle of adjusting to the son and dad syndrome, it evened out. As I listened to Earl Nightingale's Lead the Field, Brian Tracy, Dan Kennedy and Jim Rohn, these business titans, I thought, "How can I provide more value?" See, I was doing the administrative work, but that's just client maintenance.

But how can I provide value for another service and as I researched marketing I couldn't just do administrative tasks, I needed to focus on "the getting of money," as Dan Kennedy calls it. This is the most profitable skill.

As I read books on marketing of every type, it became apparent not everybody has this skill. This is why there will always be many more employees, than business owners. It is a fact of life. Marketing became like second nature.

The process: write an advertisement, post it somewhere and watch the money come in. It's an over simplification, but that's bottom-line how it works.

And I enjoyed it.

I enjoyed seeing my words, spoken or written, produce income. I knew that that was something I'd enjoy doing my entire life. Fast forward seven years to 2014 now, and I've been studying marketing for nearly seven years. I've read and studied scores of books. Not all only that, I have real world experience.

This education and experience does not happen in a classroom. This is not taking a marketing course and marketing ABC Acme Company. This is real world, real-life experience and results.

These are lessons class rooms cannot teach, only the real world can. Experiencing results triggered a thought: there are business owners throughout the country and the world who will pay for that type of service.

They're looking for somebody trustworthy, capable and dependable to take the reins of their marketing and kick it into high gear. Maybe I could offer my services to clients?

Without any further ado, I'm going to explain to you how to quickly get started in profitably marketing your business, even if you don't have two pennies to rub together.

And if you do have a marketing budget, even better, because you can experiment to see what works and what doesn't work. If it does work, ramp it up, do more of it!

Let's go.

CHAPTER 1 – Getting Started

"The secret of getting ahead is getting started."

-Mark Twain

Many small business owners throw something against the wall and hope it sticks. They don't quite know what's going to work. The first thing they typically do is copy what the business down the street does. Or copy the leader in the industry.

It's usually me too marketing. It's follow, do exactly what that guy over there has done but it's not innovation, it's not differentiation, it's not something that causes them to stand out from the thousands of advertisements that people see or hear.

It doesn't allow them to stand out. In a noisy, hectic world, you really need to stand out. You can't afford to blend in with your competition down the street and if you do, you'll quickly become one of the many business casualties.

I see this all the time. Just in my neck of the woods I see the massage place across the street recently closed down. The liquor store around the corner recently closed down. A mattress store a little further down recently closed down.

You've experienced this, too.

You've seen these small businesses, offered a great service, offered a great product, whatever type of business it was, but they failed to attract people to spend money on their service and product.

Failure to attract people with cash in hand, who raise their hand and say "that's for me," will result in you closing up shop for good. So how do you break that pattern? How do you avoid becoming one of the many business casualties?

First, identify your target market. In other words, who do you appeal to? Think about it, what's your background? Who would you like to do business with? I'll tell you that attempting to appeal to everybody, causes you to be appealing to nobody, so it's important that you first identify who you appeal to, and who you want to attract.

For example, are they homeowners? Are they renters? Do they live in the good side of town or do they live in the bad side of town? Do they earn $30,000 dollars or do they earn $300,000 dollars? Do they drive a Mercedes or do they drive a Honda? What type of hobbies do they have? Do they have a boat? Do they go on overseas vacations? Etc.

If you are an established business, think about your top five customers. What are their hobbies? What are their interests? What are their characteristics? And think of how you could clone them, not clone in the truest and purest sense of the word, but clone in the sense that you attract more people like them.

Then conduct a survey of your top five customers/clients, customers and clients, find out what they are into, find out what they are like, find out what their age ranges are.

Are they single or are they married? Do they have two kids, no kids? What nationality are they? And on and on and on. There's the demographics which is the age, the gender, the income status, the neighborhood they live in, but then there is another thing called Psychographics.

Psychographics is what Simon Sinek's book, *Start with why* refers to. Psychographics is attracting people who identify with your core beliefs. What do you believe in? What is it that drives you? What is your faith background? What is your belief in life? What's your outlook on life? It's identifying that core belief and attracting people who are of the same core belief as you.

Don't waste your time trying to convert the unconverted. Believe me, I've tried. Don't try to convince someone who is unconvinced.

If they need convincing, if they need to be sold on you and you need to spend massive amounts of time and effort getting them convinced that what you sell, your product or service, is for them, then it is better and best that you refocus your energies on someone who is already converted.

It is much easier to preach to the converted than it is to preach to the unconverted with the converted they are ready to whip out their wallets and buy from you.

With the unconverted, you would spend a fortune and they would still be unconvinced and unconverted. So preach to the choir, preach to the converted, and find the people whose core beliefs match yours.

Think about it; are you a church goer? Find more church goers, find people who are at church on Sundays. Find a way to connect with those people, find a way to connect with people who are into what you are into.

Do you believe that baseball is the greatest sport? Then find people who identify with your core values. Find more people like you and more people like your top clients/ patients/customers.

Second, identify what makes your business different. And I'm not talking about your logo or your employees or your location, that's not really it. Your USP, what is it that makes you really different? What is it that makes you different from the crowd? Think about it, is it speed?

Are you like Dominoes, where their Unique Selling Proposition (USP) was "hot pizza delivered in thirty minutes or it's free?" Is it price, like McDonald's sells their coffee based on price, cheaper coffee than Starbucks but decent tasting? Is it atmosphere?

Think about Starbucks. They charge premium prices for coffee but have attracted a massive following because it's about the experience, it's about the atmosphere. Think about Disney, it's about the experience, the atmosphere and they command premium prices.

So what is your Unique Selling Proposition? What makes you different? What have you identified as the differentiating factor in your business? And write down everything that you can think of.

Write or type it out and think of a way to make that different. In other words, answer the question that every prospect, people who have yet to do business with you, but may do business with you in the future; answer the question that every prospect has, which is, 'why should I do business with you versus any other business? Why should I choose your business?

Not 'oh, because we're a dry cleaner.' No, because your competition already provides that service. Think of your local donut shop for example, they provide doughnuts. Now think of Krispy Kreme.

Why have you heard of Krispy Kreme but your local donut shop is only local? First, Krispy Kreme has a drive through. Second, their Unique Selling Proposition is "hot glazed doughnuts now."

In other words, at particular times of the day, they'll have the "hot donuts now" sign lit and people know when that sign is up, they can walk into their local Krispy Kreme or they can go through the drive through, and they'll have hot, fresh baked, glazed donuts.

That's their unique selling proposition, it's convenience. So is it price? Is it convenience? Is it atmosphere? Another one is speed. Is it speed? You can compete on speed. You can charge a premium price for speed.

Think of a local coffee shop, when it's their prime time there's a line going through the door. But when you go to Starbucks, you can get out of the car or you can stay in the car, you don't have to go inside the Starbucks if you don't want to.

They provide convenience, a differentiating factor. So what is your USP? Why should your prospects choose you versus your competition?

Third, how will you provide that service? How do you fulfil this service? Your promise, your USP. So if it's speed, your Unique Selling Proposition is you provide print services in one day or its free, that's your USP.

Well how do you do it? Our high quality, top-notch, state-of-the-art printing presses or whatever they're called, blah blah, blah do your job.

How do you do it? How do you fulfil? How are you able to do that? Because the next thing that people are thinking about is, "that sounds too good to be true." How can you do that? How can you fulfil?

You want to be believable because many people buy into the old adage, "if it's too good to be true it probably is." So you need to be able to identify why they should believe your claim. There are many skeptical people.

I know for myself, when I see a billboard or an advertisement anywhere and it sounds too good to be true I'm thinking, "That sounds too good to be true. I'm going to stay away from that business."

Just think: if you were in the market for a Rolex, and you know that Rolex charges a premium price but some guy on the street comes up to you and says "I'm selling a Rolex for $100."

I'm sure you wouldn't believe him. You'd say, "That's a lie. There's no way that a Rolex goes for only $100. That's fake. That's phoney because it's 'too good to be true.'

At the same time, if someone said I'm selling a brand-new, fresh from the manufacture Mercedes Benz for $5000 dollars you wouldn't believe it, only because it's too good to be true.

So what is your claim? What is your USP and how do you deliver on that USP, on that promise, on that claim?

Fourth, how will they benefit? Tell them how they're going to benefit because you can have the greatest USP, you can have the most believable story, but if you don't back that up and say what you're going to do to benefit your prospect they still won't believe you. So you need to find that hidden need, find the deeper need.

In other words, when someone is in the market for a new mattress, think about it, is it because they need a new mattress? In some cases, yes. But in a lot of cases, no. What does having an uncomfortable mattress result in? One, it can can cause snoring.

Two, you get a lack of sleep. Three, that will result in irritability. Four, it will reduce job performance. Five it will prevent having a healthy interaction with loved ones and friends and co-workers, and so on. So the deeper need is not a mattress, the deeper need is, it will improve your relationships!

So if you're selling mattresses, your USP could be, "we'll deliver a custom made mattress to your door within 24 hours because our machines, our presses or whatever they're called, our mattress machines will do whatever.

They don't care how it is made, tell them "our mattress experts will design a custom made mattress within seventy two hours or your money back; don't argue with your significant other anymore. You can sleep soundly knowing your Sleep Apnea will soon be cured with one of these premium mattresses. So visit our store this Friday or Saturday!"

You're reaching down to a deeper need. It's not, 'oh you need a new mattress because you're uncomfortable', that's a basic need but you're reaching to a deeper need.

The deeper need is the relationship issues-their interaction with their supervisor, their co-workers, because they have been up at night. Because they are shaken to wake up due to them snoring to the point their spouse has been aggravated by it and is losing sleep as well.

So you're reaching to a deeper need. Reach that core need and you will succeed. I've given you some food for thought in getting started.

But what are some avenues, what are some marketing methods that you can use profitably? What are some things that you can do today even if you don't have two pennies to rub together? We'll cover that in the next chapter.

Onward!

CHAPTER 2 – Effective marketing methods you can implement today...for cheap

"Without frugality none can be rich, and with it very few would be poor."

-Samuel Johnson

Many small business owners think that if they just do what their competition is doing they will be successful.

But that's just not the case.

I've met and interacted with many small business owners who are on the brink of bankruptcy because they did exactly what their competitors, who had a much larger budget, did.

As Earl Nightingale said, 'if you want to be successful, look at what your competition is doing and do the total opposite.'

So if your competition is advertising in the Yellow Pages, then advertise on line. If your competition is advertising online then send out Direct Mail. If your competition is doing Direct Mail, you get the idea.

First, you need a website. Yes, it's probably been said many times before but you need a website, not just any website but a website that draws customers to you.

So find a cheap or free website maker. Some ideas: 1. Vista Print does it for cheap, they'll give you a thirty day trial 2. Web.com gets you started for $1.95. And there are other good ones out there. So pick one out, pick a template and get going.

Usually it would take you no more than ten to fifteen minutes. As far as the design, remember good enough is good enough. Don't worry about having your website perfect just get something up there, get something going, then you can always take corrective action along the way.

You can always improve along the way. But get something up there if you don't already have a website.

Second, get a Landing Page so when people find your website, you don't just have a glorified business card up there.

Have some type of free information they can access in exchange for their contact information, at least their name and their email address. If you can get more information like a phone number and a mailing address, all the better.

In return, offer them something valuable. Whether it's a book, an eBook, a series of training videos, a consultation, a free gift, whatever the case is, give them something in exchange.

As Bob Burg's book, *Go-Giver* says, "go-givers earn more than those who don't give." So give something in exchange for their information. Don't just ask for their information and say thank you. Give them something as a token of your appreciation. Then how's your website going to get found?

Third, set up an AdWords account. There've been books written on AdWords so I am not going into detail. If you can be successful with AdWords then you can go onto other marketing methods.

But if you are not successful with AdWords then you need to tweak your advertisement until it is successful, and find out how you can deliver on what your customers are looking for.

It's much easier to "enter the conversation in your prospect's head", as the late, great Robert Collier said, than it is to try to figure out what people are looking for.

So go to Google keyword planner and find out what they are looking for. Choose relevant keywords related to what your business offers, and then pick up Perry Marshall's Ultimate Guide to Google AdWords.

That book will give you a foundation on how to profitably set up your AdWords ads or you can contact me and I'll be glad to assist you with your google AdWords campaign.

Fourth, Direct Mail. You may have heard or read that the Post Office has cut back on their staff and their revenues have been declining, but as far as business mail, their revenues are up. That tells you something. I've noticed that I am receiving a lot less mail than I did before. But just like baseball hitting coaches teach their hitters, "hit them where they're not." Hit the ball where the fielders are not.

You want to go where your competition is not, so if your competition is not using Direct Mail then especially use Direct Mail. One nice thing about direct mail is you can test.

You can start small, as small as you'd like. You can mail fewer, you can mail twenty-five recipients four times, and find out if that works, because remember, the sale is typically made on the fifth contact or later.

Guess how many business owners quit after the first or the second or the third attempt? Yes, over ninety percent, which is why the majority of small businesses will close down within the first five years but a select few will continue going because they have learned how to market persistently. So use Direct Mail profitably.

I recommend *the Direct Mail solution* by Craig Simpson. That book will give you a foundation on how to profitably and effectively use Direct Mail, or you can contact me and I'd be more than happy to assist you with your Direct Mail campaign.

Fifth, Flyers/ Door Hangers. Use these to blanket your local area. Last I checked you, could purchase something like four thousand door hangers for $99 at ladyprinting.com, and the thing about door hangers is they automatically get read.

How do I know?

Because when I receive a door hanger, I can't help but read it as it's the first thing on my door. Before I even unlock the door, as soon as I'm putting the key into the door knob, I can't help but read it, at least look at it.

I've gotten cards from landscapers and pizza places, but you know many times they do it? You've probably guessed it, once, they do it once.

But remember, the sale is made on the fifth contact or later so if you have four thousand door hangers, identify eight hundred homes, you probably want homes, because those will likely be your best customers, Identify eight hundred homes in your local area and put a door hanger on those doors, or have someone do it, every week.

So if you distribute the door hangers on a Tuesday, do it next Tuesday and next Tuesday and next Tuesday and so forth, until they've gotten the door hanger/flyer five times.

Sixth, cold calls. Something that a lot of business owners don't like to do. How much would it cost you to get the phone book?

Yes that's old school, but the nice thing about the phone book is it gives you names, and gives you an automatic list of names that you can look up and find out the phone numbers to.

Believe it or not, peoples' numbers are still listed in there. Even though the majority of people have cell phones, there are still people who have land lines and it may have decreased significantly, but there are still people listed in the phonebook.

The law of averages says that you if do something enough times, then you'll see results. It's at play in everything that you do, every marketing method that you use.

Make enough calls and you'll see results. So pick up your local phone book, the white pages, and just start going from A to Z.

You don't want to do it? Have your kid do it or look on Craig's List or Elance or oDesk or Fiverr and ask someone to do all these calls for you, and you'll start seeing results.

Seventh, Word of Mouth networking. Tell everybody you know, about what your business offers. Use email, social media, and free business networking events in your area to connect with local business owners and individuals.

If your county has a county fair or you have a state fair that's a perfect opportunity to get out there and promote the business.

What about free local networking events or seminars and classes? Get out there and get the word out. Let people know what you offer.

Eighth, Joint Ventures. If you're a florist, why not contact local churches and ministers and let them know that if they're having funerals, weddings, quinceaneras or any events that require flowers, you'd be more than happy to provide the floral arrangement.

What about wedding planners? You're a florist, that's a perfect complement, wedding planners always need good florists. What about tuxedo shops and bridal shops? What about funeral homes? They always need flowers, you get the picture.

A business that will eventually need your services, joint venture with them, give them a percentage of the proceeds, give them a discount for their customers and you'll see a return on that.

How much will it cost you but a few minutes of your time to either go and drop off business cards and to talk with the person responsible for making those decisions or give them a call and send a thank you card with coupons for your service/product or two, three or all four of those "touches.

Call them, visit them, send them a letter and send them an email and see what that will do to business. These will get you started in the right direction.

Ninth, Craig's List. Craig's List fits in, that's absolutely free, all you need is an account and you can set up as many advertisements as you want and refresh them every other day. Will that generate business? I don't know. Try it. See if it works. It works for some business owners that I've met.

I've tested it out and it works for different type of businesses depending on your advertisement and I recommend that you have it indented, so have it stand out.

Use some kind of shapes or something that causes it to stand out even more, learn about headlines, catchy headlines that will get the reader into the body of your advertisement and get them to call. All the better if you can link your website into a landing page. All these tie in together.

Now if you're contemplating placing an advertisement in the Yellow Pages, the paper, a magazine and so forth or another print media, keep in mind print is going to be a premium price, because those publishers have print costs, production costs, employee costs, location costs, distribution costs, all kinds of costs to factor in, so I recommend effectively using marketing methods 1 through 9 **before** venturing into print ads.

So those are some foundational marketing methods that you can use to quickly market your business and generate revenue but how do you write advertisements to increase business? How do you generate advertisements and ideas to get people to respond to your marketing methods? I'm glad you asked.

Continue on to Chapter 3 to find out.

CHAPTER 3 – How to write money making advertisements even…if you flunked English

"I'm writing a book. I've got the page numbers done."

-Steven Wright

When you first think of writing, typically many people think of a writer slaving away with piles of books surrounding him, typing at the typewriter or computer, with coffee stains all over his shirt, living a hermit's life.

But when I talk about writing advertisements, I'm not talking about writing a novel or a biography or a history book, I'm talking about putting words on paper or on a website or on a marketing piece that would stimulate someone to purchase from your business.

It will stimulate someone to try your product or service. So what are some rules of thumb for writing money making advertisements?

First off, you need a catchy headline, and by catchy I don't mean necessarily deep or creative. It doesn't necessarily have to be something that Shakespeare would be proud to read. It doesn't have to be something that an English teacher would approve of, but it does need to catch attention.

So catch attention with your advertisement, with your headline. The vast majority of people, think of it, when they read the newspaper, when they look on-line for news or when they're looking anywhere for anything that interests them, whether it's news or products or services or stories, the first thing they look at is the headline, the very first thing.

The vast majority of headlines get read, so I've read and the consensus is to spend at least fifty percent of the time you spend writing your advertisement, whether it's on-line or off-line writing the headline, think that's overkill?

That's the rule of thumb, that's what the experts who have sold hundreds of millions of dollars recommend. So spend time learning good headlines. How do you learn about good headlines?

Read The National Enquirer and Cosmopolitan. Believe it or not, The National Enquirer has one of the highest subscription rates of any print media in the world, so look at the National Enquirer and Cosmopolitan.

Well how can you do that without going to your local news stand? Just Google National

Enquirer and you can read the headlines on their website.

You can also opt in for a subscription and try out a subscription your iPhone, on your iPad or on-line, that's delivered to you on a regular basis, then you can learn about it that way or you can just log in to their website where they have their headlines.

Consider how catchy those headlines are, look at how much work those writers put into crafting that catchy headline and follow their pattern then look at, do a Google search for headlines, winning headlines, look at the most successful headlines and study them.

What about them made them catch attention and follow their pattern, follow that example. For more headline resources look up John Carlton's guide, *Copywriting Secrets of a*

Marketing Rebel and pick up a book called *Tested Advertising Methods* by John Caples. These will give you some food for thought and some insight into how to write catchy headlines and proven headline templates.

The second most read part of an ad is the PS. The PS, in addition to the headline, gets read the majority of the time. Typically it goes like this, on-line or off-line people read the headline first then the PS.

So make sure that whatever your offer is, whether it's a free report or service or you're selling something or you're giving a discount, make sure you reiterate the urgency of people responding.

For example, if you have a deadline of June 30th for people to respond or the first ten to respond get that discount, or that whatever free gift you're giving away, then make sure to reiterate it in the PS.

For instance, "make sure you respond before June 30th because you wouldn't want to miss out on the free report, How to get your life back from alcohol abuse" or whatever it is you're giving away.

Reiterate that, make it as strong as possible think, how would I respond? And then think and then give your piece to your friends and relatives and co-workers and classmates, as many people as possible, the people whose opinions you trust.

Let them read it and have them read it out loud to you and ask them if they have any questions and see if it's something that they would enjoy reading or buying into.

Not reading for entertainment because remember you're not writing for entertainment, you're not writing so people can enjoy it, you're not writing for a novel, you're not writing for a magazine or a movie or a television show or radio, you're writing so people will respond, you're writing so people would buy, so remember that.

Don't write to entertain. Write to sell.

After the PS is the first sentence, also known as The Lead. I recommend the book by Michael Masterson, *Great Leads*, which will show you how to write a great lead.

This works for on-line, it works for off-line. So first is the headline, second is the PS and third is the lead because if you got them to read the headlines and they read the PS then most likely there going to read at least the first sentence.

So try to make your first sentence no more than twelve words and make your words no more than one syllable. Believe it or not, I read a study that said the average reading level of all adults is fifth grade.

Think about a nine or ten year old or a fifth grader, if they can't understand it, an adult won't get it, either. Yes, there'll always be exceptions to the rule. But even someone with a double doctorate degree will appreciate the simplicity of your message, so write simply.

For example you have, 'Have you been experiencing sleepless nights?' Have you been experiencing sleepless nights; six words, but that word experiencing you're using because most people understand what an experience is.

Now if you said 'have you been encountering sleepless nights', then some people would be stuck on that word 'encountering' and may or may not read the rest. Remember this, a confused prospect does nothing.

If they're confused about the word 'encountering' and they see your website, your landing page or your piece, whatever it is, the majority of the time, they're going to set your piece aside or click away from your landing page or website because they don't get it.

And most people are not going to take the time, especially when it's selling them something, to find out what the word encounter means.

They're just not.

Study after study, survey after survey, have proven that most people are just lazy, especially when it comes to marketing. They're not going to do the research necessary to simplify or define the word, so use words that most people understand.

Then after the Lead is to get them to read the next sentence. So your sentences make them read like a thriller movie, like you can't wait till the next thing happens, you don't know what to expect, you have no idea what's happening. Even if it's spoken, make it suspenseful.

Make it something that's quick, action-packed and flows from one sentence to the next. From one paragraph to the next let it flow. How do you do that?

Some writers recommend writing quickly just write as fast as you can. Don't think about anything. Just write as fast as you can, get it all down, then go as fast as possible then go back and edit it.

That's actually my recommendation. Just write as fast as possible, just quick, lightning fast. It doesn't matter if there are typos, if it's just a mess, if it's filled with run-on sentences, who cares, right?

You can go back and edit it later anyway, so write as fast as you can, as soon as that idea hits. You have an idea, start writing it all down.

Don't worry about getting it perfect. Don't worry about editing. Don't worry about any of that stuff. Don't worry about punctuation, nothing like that.

<u>Just write it all down.</u>

You've heard that saying, no doubt "when opportunity knocks you'd better answer because it may not knock again." That's your opportunity. Creativity has just hit you. A brainstorm has just hit you and you want to take advantage of that, so write as fast as possible; as soon as you have an idea just go with it.

I recommend talking it out, into your tablet, your IPhone or your PC, using a dictation service or a digital voice recorder. However you do it, just get it all down and keep talking or typing until you got it all, and you're good to go.

Then either edit it yourself or find someone to edit for you. There are tons of editors out there on Elance, oDesk, Craig's List, Fiverr. People who will edit something for you, a particular number of words on Fiverr for five dollars. That's something worth checking out.

So have them edit it for you, get it down to where you like it and just write and post it on your website, your landing page, and see if it works. Split test.

Split test simply means having two landing pages, websites or marketing pieces put out at the same time too, splitting up your list, so for example, if you're going to have someone put out a thousand door hangers split up the list into two lists of five hundred.

Do two different door hangers, not colours, have the colours the same, have the wording the same. Just change the headline but otherwise have everything the same because you can't test more than one thing at a time.

Otherwise you'll have skewed test results. You'll think you had a higher response rate because of your headline when it was actually due to your offer.

For example, don't have two different headlines and then your offer is one free pizza with every pizza purchased and then the other one is ten dollars off your purchase. Don't test more than one thing at a time.

For a deeper understanding of testing read Claude Hopkins' book *Scientific Advertising*, which is *the* classic book on the scientific method of advertising.

David Ogilvy, a legend in the marketing and advertising industry recommended that anyone who has anything to do with marketing shouldn't have anything to do with marketing unless they've read that book seven times.

It's short and to the point but has some nuggets that you will appreciate knowing and learning. From there you'll have a deeper understanding of testing.

So do a split test, whatever it is, you're sending a mail piece, you're doing landing pages, whatever it is, do a split test then track the results.

How do you do that with physical ad pieces or letters? Have tracking codes. Let's say you have two pieces, one says buy one pizza get one free, the other says free pizza with every purchase or something like that, then on each one have a different code.

Tell them, "mention offer code one pizza and then, the other code would be pizza one," that way when they call to order, you'd know that more results came from the one pizza piece than came in from the pizza one piece. Make sense? Okay.

Then from there your job is to figure out the winner. So whichever piece did better, let's say that you put out one thousand pieces and pizza one, that said free pizza with every purchase brought in ten customers but the buy one pizza get one free brought in fifteen customers, then you're going to want to do more of the pizza one, because you see the buy one get one free out-did the other one by fifty percent.

You say but the other one did fifteen while the other one did ten, yes, but fifty percent of ten is five and it out-did the free pizza with every purchase by five, that's, fifty percent.

So you want to do more of the buy one get one free because that means it's working, you have a hot crowd.

But you say 'okay, that's great, these are great suggestions and I'd like to do them. But I've learned the 80/20 principle: 80 percent of my results will come from 20 percent of my efforts. You're a great business student. Let's move on to

the next phase of marketing your business, which
is for established business owners.

CHAPTER 4 – How to find the gold mine right under your nose

"Opportunities are like sunrises. If you wait too long, you miss them."

-William Arthur Ward

In his talk *Acres of Diamonds*, Russell Conwell, the founder of Temple University shares a story.

There was a man who went out looking for diamonds, so he sold his farm and everything he owned to purchase a diamond mine and he mined and he mined and he mined and he mined for several years but didn't find anything.

Then, in despair, he sold the diamond mine for a few hundred dollars to a young man and went on his way.

He died penniless.

The young man on the other hand, mined for only a couple of weeks and hit the mother lode. He retired in such comfort that he lived the rest of his days like a king with plenty of money to last for generations.

So what is the moral? The moral is you're closer than you think to your mother lode, to your breakthrough and your mother lode might be sitting right under your nose.

So you are an established business, you have customers who know you and like you and trust you, who hang off of every word you say and you want to find out how to get them to do more business with you. Well I am glad that you expressed interest in this vital subject.

Here's how:

Let's say you own a restaurant. I love restaurants because they are so easy to market. The thing that most business owners, not just restaurant owners, don't understand is they don't need more customers. They need more customers buying more often.

This, my friend, is one of the main ways to grow your business.

If you can get your current customers to buy from you more often, then you can experience a doubling of your revenue this year, I guarantee it. So how do you get your customers to buy from you more often?

Let's say that you, as a restaurant owner, have customers who come in and buy a drink with their meal and they come maybe at lunchtime or dinner time and then they are gone. Well, think about this: when they come in, how can you get them to come back more often?

Have you ever been to a haircut place, a nail place or even Starbucks and they offer a rewards program? Did you know that Starbucks, last I checked, has over one million Gold Card holders?!?!

They gladly spend money at Starbucks on a daily basis for their Java Fix. Once they've purchased twelve drinks or food items, they get the next one free. I have to admit that I've been a loyal Starbucks customer for over five years.

So on full disclosure I am not attempting to advertise for them because if I were, then they should be paying me a commission for every sale that results.

Starbucks used to have it to where Gold Card Holders received free pumps, free soy, and free drink upgrades but they discontinued that in favor of customers getting a reward sooner.

Which I disagreed with because when you look at it, the customer actually saves more and if you are anything like my family we tend to like pumps, the flavored pumps which it ultimately bottom line would save us more if they'd continued the other way.

I digress.

What if you said after ten meals the customer got one free? Or what if you told customers that after five meals they get a free appetizer? What if you had a punch card? You might say, well I just never thought of that.

Well you can go on Vista Print today and get something like five hundred of those for $9.00, but just think: if you have one hundred customers who frequent your restaurant and only twenty of them buy more frequently, how much is a typical customer worth to you? $10, $15, $20?

What if 20% of your customers purchase more frequently, instead of coming once per week, they now came twice per week?

That is twenty customers let's say that they are worth $10 each to you, that is $200 extra per week that is $800 extra per month and that is $9600.00 extra per year off of a $9 investment.

Can you see why that would be a worthy $9 to spend? Or I should say invest, for sure, now you can see how you can get them, your current customers, to buy more often from you.

Now what about their birthdays? Do you know your customers' birthdays? If you said yes, then great, high five, I applaud you because 99% of businesses do not know their customers birthdays.

Starbucks knows mine; I get a free drink on my birthday. Do you know your customers' birthdays? If not, then why not?

They like you, they know you, they trust you, ask them what their birthday is, keep a database, a spreadsheet, contact management, something, and on their birthday, every month, the first of every month, say first of June, just find out all your customers whose birthdays are in June and June 1 send them a free birthday card, a postcard, a letter, something.

Can you imagine?

Let's say that you have one hundred customers who frequent your restaurant and you get all hundred of those customers' birthdays and to average out we will just say that twenty of their birthdays, to simplify, twenty of their birthdays are in June, so you send out twenty postcards, letters, whatever.

I recommend you send out a letter because it is more personal, it's like a birthday card, a lot of emails get overlooked although email is effective, but send it out because it is more personal and it shows that you care about them.

So sending out a birthday card might cost you fifty or sixty cents, but here is the kicker, okay, you give your June customers a free meal, everything included on their birthday: free appetizer, free meal, everything, the works, not this free dessert or free drink thing, that is being cheap.

Give them a $20 gift card on their birthday. You might say, "Whoa, I'm out $20. No, no, no, no, you're not my friend! Check this out, think about it for a second, think with me, let's put our heads together really quick, do you, or anyone you know go out to a meal on your birthday, alone?

Eureka!

No you don't! 99% of people **do not** go out to a meal on their birthdays alone, lunch or breakfast or dinner, regardless, most people have someone with them, at least one other person.

Now remember you have twenty customers whose birthdays are in June and you sent out twenty letters or twenty birthday cards, giving them $20 on their birthday, not a Visa gift card because you want them to spend the money with you so you give them a gift card to your restaurant.

All these June people between June 1 and June 30th, come in waving their gift cards and say, "Wow! thank you so much I really appreciate that, blah, blah, blah and so forth, you know John and Jane you're the greatest thing since sliced bread and butter and I love you to death and etc. etc. and they are just loving you.

Well John doesn't come in alone, does he? He brings his spouse, he probably has children, he probably has a mom, he probably has a sister, and maybe he has a brother, a cousin, two or three, maybe an auntie and uncle.

Now let's say that John, let's be conservative here, not get too excited, he might have a friend or co-worker, let's not get too excited, let's say that

John brings five people with him who typically, ordinarily don't come to your restaurant.

Because your restaurant is real close to work so he usually comes to eat lunch by himself or maybe with a co-worker but I think that five people who don't ever come to your restaurant, we're omitting the co-worker because the co-worker might come in with them, five people, his mom, his spouse, couple of kids and his cousin let's say, come to your restaurant.

Well now you have five new customers. Get their birthdays, get their contact information and let's omit the 2 children because obviously they live with John and don't have their own money.

But John's mom, sister, and cousin, have given you their contact information. You can follow up with them, give all of them a rewards card.

What if only John's sister starts coming to your restaurant?

John's sister is not going to come to your restaurant alone. Most likely she's going to come with John or with a co- worker or with her boyfriend. She is not going to come alone, now let's just back up for a second here.

Remember you sent out twenty birthday cards just for June that's it, just for the month of June. June's birthdays, not July, not any other month because you're experimenting, so twenty.

Let's say it cost you one dollar each, $20 investment, and you might say I am out $400 because I gave them a $20 gift card plus the $20 for postage equals $420.

Check this out. An average customer is worth $10 to you from the month of June alone, are you ready?

Each of those people generated one additional customer for your business that is twenty new people from the month of June alone.

Your $420 will effectively become a profit to you because remember, each of those twenty new customers is not going to come to your restaurant and eat alone.

So twenty, let's just say that they each spend $10 each, that's $200 but then they bring one person that's $400, it was just about breakeven for you excuse me.

What about next week? Do they come to your restaurant just once or do they come again because they love the food and the atmosphere and the service?

They'll probably come again, so now when they come the second time, that initial $420 investment is profit to you but remember you just did that for June, you still have the remaining months of the year, July through December, hmmm, interesting, don't you think?

Can you see how there is a hidden gold mine within your customer base? So that was a topic of rewards, now what about referrals? I kind of touched on that, with them bringing a friend or relative with them but do your customers have friends and relatives?

Of course they do.

What are you doing to get them to recommend people to you? How much is a new customer worth to you? If you could get, remember you have one hundred customers, if you can get just twenty of them, twenty of them to recommend your business and bring one new customer, what would that mean?

What if you gave them a free appetizer, what if you gave them a free meal, what if you gave them a free drink for every friend they referred, what if you rewarded them, what if you kept track of how many referrals they sent you?

What if they came in and John said, 'This is my sister, Jane' and Jane then came in and she said, 'Oh this is my husband, George' and then Jane and George came in and he said, 'Oh, we are celebrating our Mom's birthday.'

You see where I'm going here? For every referral they sent you for every new person they brought in now this goes beyond the level of 99% of businesses.

99% of businesses typically say, "oh great, there is a new customer but have no idea how that new customer came in. What if they got a coupon, what if they came with a friend or relative or co-worker? How did they come in?

And because this book is about small businesses, small businesses have an advantage over large corporations and that is you don't draw millions of people into your business per year, you may draw just hundreds or maybe even thousands and so you are more capable than a large corporation of tracking your customers.

So now your mission, should you choose to accept it - this message will self-destruct in 30 seconds - is to find out where people come from.

Determine which ad methods work by Tracking

How did they find out about your business? How did they hear about you?

That's the question that you should always ask of everybody who comes to your business, even if you ask them every single time, that's ok, because I can guarantee you when you ask people questions about themselves they will be more predisposed to talking to you, to opening up to you, to interacting with you because peoples favorite subject is, guess who?

Themselves!

Everybody's favorite subject is I. Everybody on the face of the earth. If you can ask someone so many questions about their hobbies or about their relatives but as soon as you start asking them questions about themselves, they can talk to you for hours and sometimes days on end.

So ask them how they heard about you even if it's every single time because then you can ramp up that marketing method.

Let's say they got your door hanger, or they got your mail, or they clicked on your Google ad then you can track that and say, "hey we haven't been really doing all that much of that advertising, we should do more of that" and then you can go from there.

But track, track where your customers come from, don't do things like the majority of small business owners do, or even like your competition does, haphazardly.

Don't guess where your customers come from. Don't assume that they came from a mailer, they may have said, 'Oh I got a flyer.' I sent out a lot of direct mail and lot of the time people said, 'Oh I got a flyer.'

I know what they are talking about because I ask them, 'How did you receive that flyer?' And they will say, 'Oh I got it in the mail.' There you go, so now I know okay that worked, I need to do more of that.

So find out how they heard about your business. Ask them, train your staff, give your staff incentives for asking them how they heard about your business because that information is gold my friend, like solid gold, like a Tiffany diamond- it's that valuable.

But like I said, most business owners don't have a clue about where their customers came from. They just say, 'Hi, how you doing, welcome.' That is great, but they don't ask them what brought them in today.

You know how many times I have gone to my local restaurant, Elephant Bar, I like Elephant Bar and I get their email coupons but can you guess how many times they have asked me what brought me in today? I will give you a hint; it is a nice round number, ZERO.

They have asked me zero times, how, why, or what brought me in today or how did I hear about the restaurant and grant you this because it is a large organization and they do things like large organizations do.

They say they have name recognition, everybody knows about them, that kind of thing. But you, on the other hand, my friend, have the advantage of being small, agile, and able to quickly shift gears if necessary.

Use testimonials to skyrocket your profits

After you've gotten some very satisfied customers, it's time to further mine them!

How's this possible, you ask? Ever heard about a new movie but were hesitant to watch it? Then your friend came along and raved about it? That friend gave you a golden bit of info we in the marketing world refer to as a testimonial.

Here's how to gather testimonials that will further boost your profits:

When you finish doing providing your product or service to a customer, if they tell you, "Thank heavens you're in business. I can't thank you enough for having my dry cleaning, tax return, etc. ready so quickly, accurately, etc.

All you need is their written permission to use their testimonial in all of your marketing. Use it on your website, in your direct mail, etc.

Gather as many testimonials as you can and use every last one of them to generate additional business! It's as simple as asking.

What if they don't automatically say anything nice about your business? No worries.

Tell them, "Mr./Mrs. Jones. I truly appreciate doing business with a pleasant person like you. If I could, I'd clone you all day long and make more customers just like you.

But I can't. So, Mr./Mrs. Jones, would you do me a favor? Most of our business comes from the nice things people say about us. Would you take a moment to write/video record/say how much you enjoy working with us?"

Then either video record them, have them say it while you write it, or ask them via e-mail or phone. You can reward them for giving a testimonial with a gift card or movie tickets. Be creative. Remember, the more testimonials you gather, the more you're viewed as a business worth giving money to!

So, go get you some testimonials!

You don't have to depend on what your competition is doing or just on mediocre results, you don't any longer have to just settle, you don't.

You have a choice in the matter; you can choose to have the business of your dreams, a business that thrives, a business that is on autopilot, a business that allows you to do what you have always dreamed of doing and were placed on this earth to do.

But that is a subject for the next and final chapter.

CHAPTER 5

What to do with your new found business success.

"Always bear in mind that your own resolution to succeed is more important than any other."

-Abraham Lincoln

You were placed on this earth for a reason.

Most people don't know why they were born but it is something that seriously interests everybody.

And when you know that you were placed on this earth for a reason, you base your decisions around that purpose. You don't allow anybody to distract you from that purpose.

Yeah you'll experience some speed bumps, some detours, some potholes and even some breakdowns along the way but that is part of the journey.

You are headed towards your ultimate purpose in life, so with your business growing like gangbusters 10%, 20%, 30%, 40% and up per year, what will you do as a result?

See people buy into you, people buy into your purpose in life and yes I have laid the groundwork for a basic understanding of marketing and how to use this to profitably market your business.

At the same time, what is it that you were placed on this earth to do? Let me ask you, if you had unlimited resources, you had unlimited money and you could do anything and knew that you were guaranteed to succeed what would it be? What would that be?

You fill in the blank. What would that be? With that new found understanding, it's time to turbo charge your life. It's time to use your business's profitability to live the life of your dreams.

See, because I believe that ultimately everybody was created in the image of God. I believe that most people, deep down inside, have this longing, this nagging to do something more than what they're doing, to be something more than what they are being right now and even to help more people than they have helped up to this point.

I believe that you have the potential for greatness beyond your wildest imagination and I also believe that you don't have to waste any more time, and you don't have to worry about being too old or too young, inexperienced, uneducated or being the wrong color or the wrong height or coming from the wrong family or any other excuse that you may have under the sun because all of them have been expressed by somebody somewhere who has overcome those limitations.

So what will you do? What will you do from there?

Is your purpose to feed starving children in Somalia? Is it to cure AIDS or cancer? What is your purpose? What would you do if you knew you couldn't fail and you had unlimited money?

What would you do?

I will share with you what I will do. I'm not quite there yet, but I will be there one day. I will help churches throughout the country purchase their own buildings.

I have come across many ministers who could not afford the down payment, whose churches were small but that is what I feel I am supposed to do with my life.

What about you? What are you going to do? How will you serve humanity? How will you, as the Carpenter from Galilee said, be the "greatest servant?" "He who wants to be the greatest among you must be the greatest servant" (Matthew 20:26).

And how will you be the greatest servant? How will you serve humanity? How will you live the life you are always meant to live? How will do that? What will that look like?

Who would you spend it with? Where would you live? What things would you do on a daily basis? How would your ideal day look? What car would you drive? How would you feel? Who would you spend your day with? What would you talk about?

All these things, think about those things and figure out what your high prize is, because the picture of success doesn't look the same for everybody.

For some, it's having two kids and being able to put them through college without going into debt. For some people, it's having no debt.

For other people, it's being able to retire comfortably and have the same standard of living they have now without having to worry about money.

For other people it is being able to travel in an RV and just travel the country. Other people, it's being able to travel the world, others, it's being able to help poor children, others, it is setting up parenting programs and educational programs.

What is it to you?

What is your definition of success, what would that look like? You living the life you were always meant to live. I hope and pray that you discover your ultimate purpose in life.

I highly recommend the book, *the Purpose Driven Life*. You can purchase it anywhere, books are sold on-line, off-line even thrift stores have it and you read it, you devour it and go through that journey with a friend, a relative, your spouse and your children and you live the life that you are always supposed to live.

Because that my friend, when all is said and done, when you have closed up shop for the day and when you are old and gray and your kids are grown, will be what you treasure.

Because the things that are done in this life are only preparation for the next. With that, I wish you good success, I will close with a blessing from the Old Testament that priests would say over the people before they dismissed them from synagogue services,

"May the Lord bless you and keep you, may the Lord cause his face to shine upon you and give you peace."

Until we meet in person on-line or otherwise, I thank you for reading this book and I hope it benefits you and other business owners you know, now and for years to come.